James

The Ghost of Ratemo

Illustrated by
Shirley Tourret

Series editor: Rod Nesbitt

Heinemann Educational Publishers
Halley Court, Jordan Hill, Oxford OX2 8EJ
a division of Reed Educational & Professional Publishing Ltd

Heinemann Educational Botswana (Publishers) (Pty) Ltd
PO Box 10103, Village Post Office, Gaborone, Botswana
Heinemann Educational Books (Nigeria) Ltd
PMB 5205, Ibadan

MELBOURNE   AUCKLAND
FLORENCE   PRAGUE   MADRID   ATHENS
SINGAPORE   TOKYO   SAO PAULO
CHICAGO   PORTSMOUTH (NH)   MEXICO
IBADAN   GABORONE   JOHANNESBURG
KAMPALA   NAIROBI

© James Ngumy 1993
First published by Heinemann International Literature
and Textbooks in 1993

British Library Cataloguing in Publication Data
A catalogue record for this book is available
from the British Library

ISBN 0 435 89171 5

The right of James Ngumy to be identified as
the author of this work has been asserted by him in accordance
with the Copyright, Designs and Patents Act 1988.

Glossary
Difficult words are listed alphabetically on page 29

Printed and bound in Great Britain by
George Over Limited, Rugby and London

Ratemo woke up early every day. His school was far away. After breakfast he ran all the way to school. He did not want to be late. After school he ran all the way home. He did not want the darkness to catch him.

On Friday when school was over, Ratemo was very happy. He did not wake up early on Saturday. He did not run to school and run back. On Saturdays he was never tired.

One Friday evening, the radio said a bank had been robbed. The bank was in the town near Ratemo's village.

That night when Ratemo fell asleep, he had a dream. He dreamed that robbers were chasing him. The dream woke him up. He fell asleep again, and had the same dream. He stayed awake until morning. Then he fell asleep again. He started to dream again. Someone was holding his shoulder.

'Go away!' shouted Ratemo. 'Leave me alone!'

'Wake up! Wake up!' someone said. Ratemo opened his eyes. He saw his father.

'Who were you fighting with?' his father asked.

'I was dreaming,' said Ratemo. 'Some robbers were chasing me. I was very frightened.'

'You're all right now,' his father said. 'It's time to get up. We have work to do. You can't sleep the whole day.'

Ratemo was still feeling sleepy. He did not want to get up. He rubbed his eyes and yawned.

'Get up now,' said his father. 'Put your shirt on.'

Ratemo got up. He went to the bathroom and washed himself quickly. The cold water made him feel better. He dressed and went to eat his breakfast.

His father's newspaper was on the table. The story about the robbers was on the front page.

Ratemo read the story carefully. The robbers had stolen a lot of money.

'Don't read the paper now,' his father said. 'Eat your breakfast. We have work to do.'

'The bank manager has promised a reward for anybody who helps to catch the robbers,' Ratemo said excitedly.

'Yes, I read that,' replied his father. 'But we can't catch robbers this morning. We have to work. Now finish your breakfast.'

Ratemo ate quickly. He was still looking at the newspaper. The photograph of the bank manager was next to the story.

'I wish I could get my photograph in the paper,' Ratemo said. 'I wish I could find those bank robbers. I'd capture them and get that reward.'

'You won't if you sit in a chair all day,' replied his father. 'Come on, it's time to go.'

Ratemo's father, who was called Osano, was a carpenter. He made chairs, tables and beds. Sometimes, when someone died, Ratemo's father made a coffin. He was very good at making coffins.

Ratemo was fourteen years old. He was in Class Seven at St Paul's Primary School. At school they learnt to make things with wood. During the holidays, Ratemo helped his father in the workshop. He was going to be a good carpenter.

Ratemo ran after his father into the workshop. His father was holding one end of a coffin.

'Help me to carry this to the pick-up,' his father said. 'We have to take it to Kamanga.' Kamanga was the next village.

'Has someone died?' asked Ratemo.

'Yes,' replied his father. 'A boy about your age. Now lift that end.'

Ratemo and his father put the coffin in the pick-up.

They got into the pick-up and Osano started the engine.

Kamanga was very far away and the road was not smooth. There were a lot of pot-holes in the road. The coffin was thrown up in the air. Then it crashed down again.

'This road is bad,' Ratemo's father said. 'The coffin will be smashed before we get to Kamanga. The people won't buy it.'

'Let me sit in the back,' Ratemo said. 'If I sit on the coffin, it won't move.'

'All right,' Osano replied, 'but be careful.'

He stopped the pick-up. Ratemo climbed into the back and sat on the coffin. The pick-up started again. It was very cold on the back of the pick-up. Then Ratemo had an idea.

'I can get into the coffin,' he thought. 'I'll be warm and the coffin won't move.'

He opened the heavy lid and got in. He pulled the lid back in place. Ratemo felt warm and comfortable. Very soon he fell asleep.

Before you reach Kamanga, there is a big forest. It is a dark, lonely place. Ratemo's father was nervous. He wanted to stop and call Ratemo back into the pick-up. But the village was not very far away, so he drove on.

Osano switched on the radio and listened to some music. Then there was a police announcement.

'Last night,' the announcer said, 'robbers broke into the City Bank. They stole a large sum of money. The police chased them, but they escaped into the forest near Kamanga village. Anyone who helps to catch the thieves will receive a reward.'

Osano looked out of the pick-up window. The forest was dark and frightening.

Suddenly Osano saw a man waving at the side of the road. Another man was lying in the road.

'Maybe these are the thieves!' Ratemo's father whispered.

Then he saw the clothes the men were wearing. They were the green uniforms of the forest rangers. Osano was not afraid any more. He stopped the pick-up.

'What's wrong?' Osano asked.

'My friend fell in the forest,' the ranger said. 'I think he's very sick.'

Ratemo's father got out of the pick-up.

'Help me put him in the back,' the ranger said. 'You take his legs and I'll take his shoulders.'

Osano bent down to lift the sick man's legs. Then he heard footsteps behind him. Before he could look up, something hit him on the head. He fell, unconscious. More men came out of the forest.

'We're lucky,' one of them said. 'Now we can escape.'

'Pull this man into the bush,' another man said. 'Then take off those uniforms and get into the pick-up. We must get away.'

One of the men looked in the back of the pick-up.

'Aaaaah!' he screamed. 'There's a coffin in here.'

'There is a coffin?' said another.

'Yes, and there's a dead body in it,' the first man said. He was looking through the little window in the lid of the coffin.

'That's good luck too,' the leader said.

The others looked surprised. How could a coffin with a dead man be good luck?

'What do you mean? How are we lucky?' the man in the pick-up said.

'We can pretend that the dead body is a relative,' the leader replied. 'The police might stop us. We can tell them we are going to bury the body. You must all look very sad. Now let's get in the pick-up.'

All the other men looked frightened.

'I don't want to sit with a dead man,' one of them said.

'Climb in the back and look sad,' the leader ordered. 'If you don't, I'll kill you.'

Three men sat in the front. The others sat in the back with the coffin. They were all afraid and they were very quiet.

The leader started the engine and drove off.

The police stopped the pick-up outside Kamanga village. A police Inspector spoke to the leader. He was carrying a pistol.

'What have you got in the back?' he asked.

The leader looked very sad. He pretended to be crying.

'A relative has died,' he said. 'We're going to bury him. His body is in a coffin in the back.'

'Let me see the coffin,' the Inspector said. He did not believe the leader's story.

The policemen went to the back of the pick-up. The robbers were looking very sad. The coffin lay on the floor between them.

'Are you sure there is a dead body in the coffin?' asked the Inspector.

'Oh yes, sir,' said the leader. 'Quite dead, sir. Look through this little window.' He pointed to the coffin lid.

The robbers pushed the coffin towards the back of the pick-up.

Ratemo woke up when he felt the coffin move. Then he heard the voices. He thought the pick-up was in the village. He pushed at the lid of the coffin and sat up.

'Ooooooooh! Aaaaaaah!' screamed the robbers.

'There's a ghost in the coffin,' shouted one of them. He jumped off the pick-up. The others jumped after him. They ran as fast as they could.

'Stop or I'll shoot,' shouted the Inspector, lifting his pistol.

The robbers ran faster. The policeman fired into the air.

'Stop!' he shouted again.

The other policemen pointed their rifles.

'Arrest them!' the Inspector told his men.

The Inspector then spoke to Ratemo.

'Where did these men find you?' he asked Ratemo.

'Where's my father?' Ratemo asked, looking all around.

'Your father?' The Inspector was surprised. 'Is he one of these men?'

Ratemo got out of the coffin. He looked at the robbers. They were all strangers.

'No!' said Ratemo. 'My father was driving the pick-up when we started. We were taking the coffin to Kamanga. I got into the coffin and fell asleep. I don't know any of these people. What has happened to my father?' Ratemo was frightened.

'I don't know,' said the Inspector, 'but these men will tell us.' He walked over to the robbers.

'Where did you leave the owner of this pick-up?' he asked. 'Tell me at once or I'll get very tough.' He put his hand on his pistol.

The robbers all started to talk at once. The Inspector put them in a police lorry and they drove back along the road.

They soon found Ratemo's father. They also found the money from the bank. The robbers had hidden it in the forest.

'Well,' said the Inspector to Ratemo and Osano, 'there's a big reward waiting for you at the police station.'

'A reward? What for?' asked Ratemo. He was very excited.

'For helping us to catch these thieves,' said the Inspector. 'These are the robbers who broke into the bank last night.'

'How did I help you to catch them?' asked Ratemo. 'They were going to get away when you stopped them.'

'That's true,' said the Inspector. 'But I was going to let them go, to bury you. You came back to life in time. You helped a lot. These people are really bad. We've been looking for them for a long time. Now let's go to the station.'

When Ratemo and Osano reached the station, they had to tell their story again. Soon newspaper reporters and photographers came. They told Ratemo to get into the coffin. They wanted to see how he frightened the robbers. They took a lot of pictures.

'Will the pictures be in the newspaper?' Ratemo asked the Inspector. The Inspector just smiled.

The next morning Ratemo's father brought home a newspaper.

On the front page was a picture. It showed Ratemo getting out of the coffin. Under the picture were the words:

RATEMO'S GHOST CATCHES BANK THIEVES

Ratemo was very happy. That afternoon a messenger brought a letter for Osano. He read it and then started to smile.

'Come on, son,' he said. 'We're going to receive a reward for Ratemo's ghost.'

Questions

1 Why does Ratemo have a bad dream?
2 Why do Ratemo and Osano have to go to Kamanga?
3 The thieves were wearing forest rangers' uniforms. How do you think they got the uniforms?
4 Why did Osano stop when he saw the men were forest rangers?
5 How did the robbers plan to escape from the police?
6 Explain why the police inspector said the reward should go to Ratemo.
7 Explain why the headline in the newspaper said:
   RATEMO'S GHOST CATCHES BANK THIEVES
How can a ghost catch thieves?

Activities

1 What is the difference between a pick-up, a van and a lorry? Draw a picture of each of these vehicles.
2 Write a short story about a nightmare (a bad dream) you have had. Can you explain why you had the dream?

Glossary

announcement (page 12) telling people something important using the radio or the newspapers
coffin (page 7) a wooden box for carrying a dead body
pot-holes (page 9) round holes in the road
reporters (page 26) people who report the news for newspapers or television
smooth (page 9) very flat and even
unconscious (page 14) knocked out

The Junior African Writers Series is designed to provide interesting and varied African stories both for pleasure and for study. There are five graded levels in the series.

Level 2 is suited to readers who have been studying English for four to five years. The content and language have been carefully controlled to increase fluency in reading.

Content The plots are simple and the number of characters is kept to a minimum. The information is presented in small, manageable amounts and the illustrations reinforce the text.

Language Reading is a learning experience, and although the choice of words is carefully controlled, new words, important to the story, are also introduced. These are contextualised, recycled through the story and explained in the glossary. They also appear in other stories at Level 2.

Glossary Difficult words which learners may not know and which are not made clear in the illustrations have been listed alphabetically at the back of the book. The definitions refer to the way the word is used in the story and the page reference is for the word's first use.

Questions and Activities The questions give useful comprehension practice and ensure that the reader has followed and understood the story. The activities develop themes and ideas introduced and can be done as pairwork or groupwork in class, or as homework.

Resource material Further resources are being developed to assist in the teaching of reading with Jaws titles.

Other Jaws titles at Level 2

Kagiso's Mad Uncle, Keith Whiteley, 0 435 89164 2

The Magic Pool, Gaele Mogwe, 0 435 89166 9

Masquerade Time, Cyprian Ekwensi, 0 435 89165 9

The Picture that Came Alive, Hugh Lewin, 0 435 89167 7

The Angel Who Wore Shoes, Dan Fulani, 0 435 89172 3